# 'TE
# G
# RECIPES

Meringues
Omelettes
Soufflés
Savouries
Light Snacks
and
Supper Dishes

SALMON

# Index

Anchovy Eggs   27
Baked Cheese Soufflés   16
Breton Eggs   40
Cheese Eggs   32
Coconut Macaroons   6
Cornflour Meringue Pudding   47
Crab Soufflé   46
Cream Eggs   14
Curried Eggs   5
Custard Tarts   37
Duchess Eggs   7
Egg & Cheese Pie   45
Egg & Creamed Peas   42
Egg & Herring Snack   11
Egg & Shrimp Croquettes   21
Egg Custard   31
Eggs Florentine   35

Eggy Bread   34
French Omelette   8
Friar's Omelette   39
Gold Cake   30
Ham Toasts   10
Mariner's Omelette   15
Meringues   24
Pancakes   13
Pickled Eggs   38
Portuguese Eggs   19
Savoury Baked Eggs   43
Scotch Eggs   23
Soufflé Omelette   3
Spanish Omelette   29
Stuffed Savoury Pancakes   26
Sweet Omelette   18
Tuna Egg Salad   22

Cover pictures *front:* "Dinnertime" by *Walter Hunt*   *back:* "Friends" by *Edwin Bottomley*
*title page*: "Feeding Time" by *Henry Yeend King RBA*

Printed and Published by J. Salmon Ltd., Sevenoaks, England © Copyright

# Soufflé Omelette

*This sweet omelette is the simplest form of soufflé to prepare and makes a rich and satisfying dessert. Use a frying pan which can be put into the oven.*

**3 egg yolks    4 egg whites    1 oz caster sugar    ½ oz butter**
**3 or 4 tablespoons blackcurrant jam (or as preferred)**
**Icing sugar to decorate**

Set oven to 350ºF or Mark 4. Beat the egg yolks and sugar together in a large bowl until creamy. In another bowl whisk the egg whites until soft and then carefully fold into the yolk mixture. Melt the butter in a suitable pan and, when sizzling hot, spoon in the egg mixture and spread out. Leave in the pan for about 1 minute to cook the bottom of the omelette and then transfer to the oven for a further 8 to 10 minutes or until just set. Spoon the jam over half the omelette, fold over the other half with a slice and dust very well with icing sugar. Transfer to a warm plate to serve. Serves 2 to 3.

'Farmyard Companions' *by J. F. Herring Snr.*

# Curried Eggs

*A mixture of fried onions and apple with cream and hard boiled eggs, served with boiled rice.*

| | |
|---|---|
| **8 hard boiled eggs** | **2 tablespoons flour** |
| **2 oz butter** | **8 fl.oz milk** |
| **2 onions, finely chopped** | **2 tablespoons double cream** |
| **1 apple, peeled, cored and chopped** | **Salt and pepper** |
| **1 clove garlic, crushed** | **Raisins and almonds to decorate** |
| **2 teaspoons curry powder (or to taste)** | **Boiled long grain rice to accompany** |

Hard boil the eggs for 10 minutes and put into cold water to cool. Remove the shells. Meanwhile, melt the butter in a pan and gently cook the onion, apple and garlic to soften. Stir in the curry powder and flour and continue cooking for another minute. Remove from the heat and stir in the milk. Return to a low heat and cook for a further few minutes stirring, to thicken the sauce. Stir in the cream, season, add the hard boiled eggs and reheat thoroughly. Serve on warm plates, sprinkled with raisins and almonds and with a border of cooked rice. Serves 4.

# Coconut Macaroons

*These simple and more-ish little macaroons are delicious with a cup of coffee or at teatime. They keep well.*

**3 egg whites**     **3 oz desiccated coconut**
**6 oz icing sugar**    **Pinch of salt**

Set oven to 300º F or Mark 2. Sift the icing sugar into a bowl. In another bowl, beat the egg whites until they hold their peaks then fold in the sifted sugar and mix in the coconut and a pinch of salt. Cover a baking sheet with non-stick silicon baking paper and drop on it teaspoons of the mixture, at least 1 inch apart. Put the baking sheet in the bottom of the oven and leave for about 20 to 30 minutes until the macaroons are dried out and light brown. When cold, carefully peel off the baking paper. Store in an airtight tin.

# Duchess Eggs

*Cheesy flavoured mashed potatoes are the foundation of this simple dish.*

| | |
|---|---|
| **5 eggs** | **Salt and pepper** |
| **1 lb mashed potatoes** | **Yolk of egg for glazing** |
| **1 oz butter** | **Tomato sauce** |
| **1 oz Cheddar cheese, grated** | **Chopped parsley to garnish** |

Boil 1 lb peeled potatoes and mash. Set oven to 375° F or Mark 5. Add one of the eggs, the butter and grated cheese to the mashed potatoes, season and combine well together. Divide the mashed potato mixture into 4 parts, shape into bird's nests and arrange in a buttered ovenproof dish. Brush with yolk of egg and put into the oven for about 10 minutes to brown. When browned, carefully break one egg into each nest and return to the oven to set. To serve, pour tomato sauce around the dish and garnish with chopped parsley. Serves 4.

# French Omelette

*This is the basic omelette to which may be added savoury fillings to individual choice or from whatever ingredients are to hand.*

**4 eggs   1 dessertspoon water   Salt and pepper
Good pinch finely chopped parsley   ½ oz butter**

Beat the eggs together lightly in a bowl and mix in the water, seasoning and chopped parsley. Melt the butter in an omelette pan and heat until really hot but not browning. Pour in the eggs and stir quickly on top, avoiding going through the mixture to the pan. As the edge begins to set, push back gently to allow raw mixture to flow in. Continue pushing back until the omelette is just cooked. Fold in three and serve at once on a hot plate. Add any savoury filling required before the first fold. Serves 2.

**Fillings:** The range of fillings is legion but the following ideas may be helpful; fillings should always be warm before adding to the omelette. Asparagus tips boiled and tossed in butter. Petit Pois boiled lightly and tossed in butter. Mushrooms diced, seasoned and fried in butter. Tomatoes blanched, skins and seeds removed, chopped and heated in butter. Ham finely chopped and heated in butter with chopped parsley.

'A Stable Interior' by E. J. Verboeckhoven

# Ham Toasts

*A useful way to produce a tasty snack with ham, cream,
hot buttered toast and lightly scrambled eggs.*

**8 eggs   2 tablespoons double cream   8 oz ham, finely chopped
4 slices of bread, toasted, buttered and kept warm
1 oz butter   2 tablespoons milk   Salt and black pepper
Parsley sprigs to garnish**

Put the cream and chopped ham into a saucepan over a low heat and heat thoroughly. When ready, spread the mixture on to the buttered toast, set aside and keep warm. Next, melt the butter in a saucepan. Beat the milk and eggs together, season to taste and add to the melted butter, stirring until the egg mixture is lightly scrambled. Pile on to the ham mixture on the slices of toast and serve at once, garnished with parsley sprigs. Serves 4.

# Egg and Herring Snack

*Hard boiled eggs covered with a tasty topping of mashed herrings, tomatoes and grilled cheese.*

| | |
|---|---|
| **4 hard boiled eggs** | **Salt and pepper** |
| **8 oz tomatoes, skinned & sliced** | **3 oz Cheddar cheese, grated** |
| **190 gm tin herrings in tomato sauce** | **Sprigs of watercress to garnish** |

Hard boil the eggs for 10 minutes and put in cold water to cool. Blanch the tomatoes in boiling water, remove the skins and cut into thin slices. Shell the eggs, cut in half lengthways and remove the yolks. Put the yolks into a basin, mash with a fork, add the herrings and mix well. Season to taste. Arrange the egg whites in an ovenproof dish, fill with the herring mixture, arrange the tomato slices around the edge and sprinkle all over with the grated cheese. Cook under a moderately hot grill until the cheese is bubbling and the eggs and fish mixture are heated through. Garnish with sprigs of watercress. Serves 4.

'Calves at a Trough' *by Walter Hunt*

# Pancakes

*Pancakes originated in the Middle Ages as a way of using up ingredients before the beginning of the Lenten fast. They are best served and eaten immediately after they have been made.*

**3 eggs    3 oz flour    Pinch of salt    ½ pint milk**
**1 to 2 oz melted butter    Lard for frying**
**Lemon juice and caster sugar    Lemon slices for decoration**

Sift the flour and salt together into a bowl. Make a well in the centre and add the eggs, beating well. Then gradually stir in the milk, beating until a smooth, creamy batter is formed. Leave the batter to stand in a cool place for 10 to 15 minutes. Grease an omelette or frying pan with lard and heat until really hot. Stir the melted butter into the batter and spoon in enough batter to coat the pan lightly. Cook for about ½ minute until lightly set on top and golden underneath, then toss or turn with a palette knife to cook the topside. Cooking only takes about 1 minute. Sprinkle the pancake with lemon juice and sugar, roll up or fold into a triangle and serve immediately from the pan, decorated with a slice of lemon. Make the remainder of the pancakes in the same way, serving them piping hot. Serves 4.

# Cream Eggs

*A simple starter; an egg mayonnaise mixture on shredded lettuce hearts.*

**3 hard boiled eggs**  
**3 oz cooked ham, finely diced**  
**1 small green pepper, diced**  
**¼ pint double cream**  
**3 tablespoons mayonnaise**  
**Pinch of curry powder**  
**Salt and pepper**  
**Crispy lettuce heart(s)**  
**Paprika pepper and chopped parsley to garnish**

Hard boil the eggs for 10 minutes and put into cold water to cool. Remove the shells and chop the whole eggs. Dice the ham and green pepper, discarding the core and seeds. Put the cream into a bowl and whisk until it just holds its shape, then add the mayonnaise and curry powder and season. Carefully fold in the chopped eggs and the ham and green pepper. Shred the lettuce heart(s) finely, arrange in individual sundae glasses or pretty bowls, pile on the egg mixture and sprinkle with paprika and chopped parsley. Serves 4.

# Mariner's Omelette

*A simple supper dish combining smoked haddock and cheese,
baked in a mixture of beaten eggs.*

**4 eggs, beaten   1 fillet smoked haddock (for 2 or 3 people)
3 oz Cheddar cheese, diced   Black pepper**

Set oven to 350°F or Mark 4. Beat the eggs together in a bowl. Remove the skin from the haddock and cut the flesh into small pieces. Cut the cheese into small pieces similarly. Put the fish and cheese into the beaten eggs, season with pepper and mix well together. Grease a shallow ovenproof dish. Pour in the egg mixture and bake in the oven for about 5 to 10 minutes until bubbling hot and the cheese is melted. Serve with mashed potatoes. Serves 2 to 3.

# Baked Cheese Soufflés

*A rich savoury dish of individual cheese soufflés baked and then returned to the oven and re-baked in a cream sauce.*

**4 egg yolks    5 egg whites**
**½ pint milk    Slice of onion    Pinch ground nutmeg**
**2 oz butter    2 oz flour    ½ teaspoon English mustard powder**
**6 oz Cheddar cheese, grated    Salt and pepper    12 fl.oz single cream**

Set oven to 350º F or Mark 4.  Butter 6 teacups.  First make a white sauce.  Heat the milk gently in a pan with the onion and nutmeg to infuse and then strain.  Melt the butter in a pan, stir in the flour and mustard powder and cook for 1 minute.  Remove from the heat and gradually stir in the strained milk, then return to the heat to thicken, stirring continuously. When thickened remove from the heat,  stir in 4 oz of the cheese and the egg yolks and season.  Whisk the egg whites until stiff then fold in to the cheese mixture.  Fill about ⅔ of each cup with the mixture and cook in the oven in a *bain marie* of boiling water for about 15 minutes until risen and set.  Allow to subside and cool.  Butter a shallow ovenproof dish.  Turn out the soufflés, arrange in the dish and sprinkle over the remaining cheese.  Season the cream with salt and freshly ground black pepper and pour over the soufflés.  Bake for about 10 minutes until golden.  Serves 6.

'The Duck Pond' *by Evert Pieters*

# Sweet Omelette

*A delicately orange-flavoured and creamy omelette sweetened with honey.*

**2 large eggs, separated     1 tablespoon double cream**
**1 small orange                    1 dessertspoon clear honey**
**A 'walnut' of butter**

Grate the rind from half the orange, then cut the orange in half and set aside the rind and the ungrated half. Squeeze the juice from the grated half. Whip the cream stiffly, then fold in the orange juice and the honey. Set aside in the refrigerator. Separate the eggs and whisk the whites in a bowl until they stand in soft peaks. Beat the yolks in another bowl. Melt the butter in an omelette pan. Fold the egg yolks into the egg whites and, when the butter is sizzling, pour the mixture into the pan. Cook for about 2 minutes, lifting the edges of the omelette away from the side of the pan as it cooks, until set. Spoon the cream mixture on to half the omelette and fold the other half over. Carefully transfer to a warm plate and serve at once, sprinkled with grated orange rind and accompanied by the remaining orange, cut into segments. Serves 1 or 2.

# Portuguese Eggs

*Fried tomatoes and onions baked with Parmesan cheese give this supper dish a somewhat Mediterranean flavour.*

| | |
|---|---|
| **4 hard boiled eggs** | **Salt and pepper** |
| **Butter and olive oil for frying** | **1 oz fresh white breadcrumbs** |
| **1 large onion, sliced** | **1 oz grated Parmesan cheese** |
| **8 oz tomatoes, skinned & sliced** | **Butter for dotting** |

Set oven to 375° or Mark 5. Hard boil the eggs for 10 minutes and put into cold water to cool. Remove the shells and cut the whole eggs into slices. Meanwhile, heat a little butter and oil in a pan and fry the onion slices until soft but not browned. Blanch the tomatoes in boiling water, remove the skins and seeds and chop into small dice. Add to the onions in the pan, season and continue cooking for a little until the tomatoes are softened. Grease an ovenproof dish and arrange the egg slices over the base. Spread the onion/tomato mixture over the eggs, cover with breadcrumbs and sprinkle over the grated cheese. Dot with butter and bake for about 10 minutes until heated through and the cheese is bubbling. Serves 3 to 4.

'The Noonday Rest' *by J. F. Herring Snr.*

# Egg and Shrimp Croquettes

*These crisp and tasty fried cakes make a nice snack or a light meal served with chips.*

**2 hard boiled eggs    1 oz butter    1 oz flour    ½ pint milk**
**2-3 thick slices white bread, crusts removed**
**½ pint shelled shrimps    Salt and pepper**
**Seasoned flour    1 beaten egg    Dried breadcrumbs    Oil for frying**
**Parsley sprigs to garnish**

Hard boil the eggs for 10 minutes then put into cold water to cool. Remove the shells. First make a white sauce. Melt the butter in a pan, stir in the flour and cook for 1 minute. Remove from the heat and gradually stir in the milk, then return to the heat to thicken, stirring continuously. Put the bread, hard boiled eggs, shrimps and white sauce into a food processor, season well and blend all together into a smooth paste. Leave in the refrigerator for about 30 minutes to cool and stiffen. When ready, form into 8 shapes with the hands and coat with seasoned flour and then with beaten egg and breadcrumbs. Fry in shallow or deep fat until crisp and golden brown. Drain on kitchen paper and serve with chips or garnish with sprigs of parsley. Serves 4.

# Tuna Egg Salad

*A hard boiled egg salad served with a creamy tuna mayonnaise; something different for a cold light repast.*

**6 hard boiled eggs**     **Grated lemon rind**
**4 oz tinned tuna, sieved**     **Salt and pepper**
**8 fl. oz mayonnaise**     **A little cream**
**Chopped chives or parsley (optional)**

Hard boil the eggs for 10 minutes and put into cold water to cool. Meanwhile, sieve the tuna (drain if necessary) and add to the mayonnaise with the grated lemon rind and salt and pepper to taste. Add a little cream and mix all together well with chopped chives or parsley (if desired). Shell the hard boiled eggs, arrange on a bed of crisp lettuce leaves and coat the eggs with the sauce. Accompany with sliced tomatoes, peppers and/or celery as preferred. Serves 4 to 6.

# Scotch Eggs

*This popular snack makes a cold meal in itself or it can be served hot,*
*with tomato sauce or cold with salad.*

**4 hard boiled eggs**  **1 oz seasoned flour**
**12 oz pork sausagemeat**  **1 beaten egg**
**2 teaspoons finely chopped parsley**  **Dried breadcrumbs**
**Vegetable oil for deep frying**

Hard boil the eggs for 10 minutes and put into cold water to cool. Remove the shells. Meanwhile, put the sausagemeat in a bowl, add the chopped parsley and mix well; hands are best. Coat the eggs with the seasoned flour and cover completely with a layer of sausagemeat; clean wet hands help to mould it evenly. Dip the coated eggs in the beaten egg and roll in the breadcrumbs to cover completely. Fry in deep fat until golden brown. Drain well on kitchen paper and serve hot or cold. Serves 4.

# Meringues

*Home-made meringues are different from the shop-bought variety and are always popular. They keep well and the same mixture can be used to create a variety of delicious desserts.*

**Egg whites    Caster sugar**
**For each egg white use 2 oz caster sugar**

Set oven to 300°F or Mark 2. Ensure the mixing bowl is absolutely clean and dry before using. Put as many egg whites are as required in the bowl and beat with an electric whisk to form soft peaks. Test by turning the bowl upside down; the whites should stay put. It is essential not to let any egg yolk whatever enter the mixture. Gradually add the sugar, a little at a time, whisking continuously while doing so. This produces really stiff whites which hold their peaks. Cover a baking sheet with non-stick silicon baking paper and place mounds of the mixture of the size desired, about ½ inch apart, on the paper using 2 metal spoons. Put the baking sheet in the bottom of the oven and leave for about 2 to 3 hours until the meringues are firm and dry. To ensure really slow drying it may be necessary to leave the oven door ajar. Allow to cool before removing from the paper.

'A Corner of the Farm' *by Walter Hunt*

# Stuffed Savoury Pancakes

*These filled pancakes can be served either as a supper dish or as a first course or a starter.*

**1 pint prepared pancake batter (see page 13)**
**½ pint prepared white sauce, well seasoned and rather thick**
**½ lb cooked chicken or ham, finely chopped or a mixture of both**
**1 oz butter   2 oz mushrooms, sliced   1 small onion, finely sliced   Salt and pepper**
**Lard for frying   2 oz Cheddar cheese, grated**

First make the batter and the white sauce. Put the chopped meat in a bowl. Melt the butter in a pan and lightly fry the mushrooms. Drain well and add to the meat. Fry the onion in the remaining butter until soft and add to the meat. Stir in the white sauce and combine well, seasoning as necessary. Transfer to a saucepan and heat through until almost boiling. Grease an omelette or frying pan with lard and heat until really hot. Using the pancake batter, spoon in enough to coat the pan lightly. Cook for about ½ minute until lightly set on top and golden underneath, then toss or turn with a palette knife to cook the topside. Cooking only takes about 1 minute. Put a tablespoon of the white sauce mixture on to one half of the pancake and roll up tightly. Place in a hot dish and keep warm. Make the remainder of the pancakes in the same way, arranging them side by side on the dish. Sprinkle over the grated cheese and put under a hot grill for 1 or 2 minutes until the cheese is melted and bubbling and the pancakes heated through. Serves 4 to 6.

# Anchovy Eggs

*A neat and well-flavoured starter or can be served as a light supper dish with a mixed salad.*

**Hard boiled eggs (as required)**    **Cayenne pepper**
**½ oz butter, softened, for 2 eggs**    **Tomatoes, thinly sliced**
**Anchovy essence**    **Brown bread and butter**
**Chopped parsley and watercress sprigs to garnish**

Hard boil the eggs for 10 minutes and put into cold water to cool. Remove the shells. Cut off a small piece from both ends of each egg to allow them to stand up, then cut in half crossways and remove the yolks. Put the yolks into a bowl with ½ oz butter for each 2 yolks, add sufficient anchovy essence and cayenne pepper to taste and mix together. Salt may not be needed, but can be added if desired. Butter thin slices of brown bread and cut into rounds or use a pastry cutter or thin-edged glass to punch out. Place a thin slice of tomato on each round of bread, stand half an egg on top and refill each egg with the mixture. Sprinkle with chopped parsley and garnish with sprigs of watercress.

'Feeding the Hens' *by W. J. Martens*

# Spanish Omelette

*This is a flexible recipe in which many vegetables that are available and which are to hand can be used.*

**4 eggs, beaten   About 2 medium size potatoes or a few small new potatoes**
**3 tablespoons olive oil   1 onion, chopped   1 clove of garlic, chopped**

Peel or scrub the potatoes and slice thinly. Heat 2 tablespoons of oil in a large frying pan. Put the potato slices in the pan with the onion and garlic. Cover the pan and cook until the potatoes are tender, turning them occasionally. Beat the eggs lightly in a large bowl. When the potato and onion mixture is cooked, add it to the bowl and mix together. Put the other tablespoon of oil in the pan and turn the heat down as low as it will go. Pour the egg, onion and potato mixture into the pan. The essence of this dish is slow cooking and it should take about 20 minutes. When there is little liquid left, turn the omelette over. It should need about another 2 minutes cooking. Or, to avoid having to turn the pan over, and if a grill is available, sprinkle some grated cheese on the surface of the omelette and put the pan under the grill until the omelette is golden brown on top. Serves 4.

In addition to potato and onion, many other vegetables may be added, as preferred i.e. tomatoes, mushrooms, peppers, peas, etc. Chop them as appropriate and add to the pan after the onion and potato have fried for a little while.

# Gold Cake

*Egg yolks can often be left over when cooking, especially after making meringues and it is useful to know what to do with them. This light textured plain cake is one answer.*

**3 egg yolks**  **5 fl.oz milk**
**2 oz butter, softened**  **6 oz flour**
**5 oz caster sugar**  **2 teaspoons baking powder**
**1 teaspoon vanilla essence**

Set oven to 350ºF or Mark 4.  Grease and line a 6 inch cake tin.  Cream together the butter and sugar in a bowl until light and fluffy.  Beat in the egg yolks with the vanilla essence and a little milk.  Sift the flour and baking powder together, stir into the egg mixture alternately with the milk, a little at a time and beat well.  Put into the tin and bake for 35 to 45 minutes until well risen and golden brown and a skewer inserted comes out clean.  Turn out on a wire rack to cool.  As a variation, the grated rind and juice of ½ a lemon or ½ an orange could be substituted for the vanilla essence.

# Egg Custard

*Another way of using up egg yolks is to make an egg custard; much nicer than a ready-mix powder.*

**3 egg yolks**                **Small piece of lemon rind**
**½ pint full cream milk**     **1 tablespoon sugar**
**1 teaspoon cornflour**

Put the milk and lemon rind in a pan and bring to the boil. As soon as the milk boils reduce the heat and simmer to allow the lemon rind to infuse for about 15 minutes. Meanwhile, well beat the egg yolks in a bowl, add the sugar and cornflour and mix thoroughly. Strain the boiled milk into the egg mixture, stirring continuously. Put back into the pan, set it over another pan of boiling water and stir the mixture continuously until it thickens. Do not let it boil. When ready, pour into a serving jug and stir again.

# Cheese Eggs

*This is a cheese-covered alternative to the ubiquitous sausage-wrapped Scotch Egg, which makes a change and is suitable for vegetarians.*

**4 hard boiled eggs**  
**4 oz Cheddar cheese, grated**  
**2 eggs, beaten separately**  
**Salt and pepper**  
**Fresh white breadcrumbs**  
**Dried brown breadcrumbs**  
**Vegetable oil for deep frying**

Hard boil the eggs for 10 minutes and put into cold water to cool. Remove the shells. Meanwhile, in a bowl, mix the grated cheese with 1 beaten egg, season and then mix in sufficient white breadcrumbs to make a pliable dough. Put into the refrigerator to rest for about 30 minutes. When required, roll out the cheese dough on a lightly floured surface to about ¼ inch thick, divide into 4 portions and wrap and mould around each egg. Dip the coated eggs in the second beaten egg and roll them in the brown breadcrumbs to cover completely. Fry in deep fat until golden brown. Drain well on kitchen paper and serve hot or cold. Serves 4.

'Kept at Bay' *by William Weekes*

# Eggy Bread

*An old fashioned and ever popular breakfast dish; or it can be quickly prepared as a standby at any time.*

**3 eggs**  
**2 tablespoons milk (optional)**  
**Tomato or brown sauce, to taste**  
**Salt and pepper**  
**4 thick slices white bread**  
**Butter for frying**

Beat together the eggs, milk (if required), sauce (to taste) and salt and pepper. Cut the slices of bread into quarters. Soak each piece of bread in the egg mixture and coat well. Heat sufficient butter in a large frying pan and fry the soaked bread squares until golden brown, turning over once. Any spare egg mixture should be poured over the bread as it is fried. Serve with crisply fried bacon for breakfast, or as a snack. Serves 4.

# Eggs Florentine

*Eggs arranged on a base of spinach and cheese with cream and baked in the oven.*

**4 eggs   2 oz butter**
**8 oz approx. chopped cooked spinach**
**2 tablespoons grated Parmesan cheese**
**3 tablespoons single cream   ½ teaspoon lemon juice**
**Salt and black pepper**

Set oven to 325°F or Mark 3. Melt the butter in a suitable ovenproof dish. Mix together the spinach, cheese, cream and lemon juice and arrange evenly over the bottom of the dish. Season to taste. Break each egg carefully into a cup and transfer to the top of the spinach mixture without breaking. Bake for about 10 to 12 minutes until the eggs are just set. Serves 4.

'Farmyard Neighbours' *by J. F. Herring Jnr.*

# Custard Tarts

*Baked custard is easy to make and individual custard tarts are always a favourite.*

**12 oz shortcrust pastry     8 fl.oz milk**
**2 large eggs     1 oz caster sugar**
**Grated nutmeg**

Set oven to 400°F or Mark 6. Grease deep patty tins or individual Yorkshire pudding tins. Roll out the pastry thinly on a floured surface and use to line the tins. Prick the bases with a fork, line with crumpled greaseproof paper, fill with baking beans and bake blind for 10 to 12 minutes. Remove the paper and beans, return to the oven to finish baking then allow to cool. Reduce oven to 350°F or Mark 4. Break the eggs into a bowl, add the milk and sugar and mix well with a fork – do not whisk the eggs. Pour the mixture into the pastry cases, grate nutmeg over the top of each tart and bake for 15 to 20 minutes until set. Leave in the tin to cool before turning out.

# Pickled Eggs

*A useful standby to keep in the larder to serve with cold meats and salad or with cold poultry or game.*

**8 hard boiled eggs**     **¼ oz black peppercorns**
**1 pint white vinegar**     **¼ oz allspice berries**
**¼ oz root ginger, lightly bruised**

Hard boil the eggs for 10 minutes and put into cold water to cool. Remove the shells. In a saucepan, simmer the vinegar and spices together for 5 minutes. Put the eggs into a warmed sterilized jar and pour the hot vinegar mixture over to cover, leaving in the spices. Seal and store in a cool dry place for about 2 weeks to allow the pickled eggs to mature.

# Friar's Omelette

*The name of this dish is nothing to do with a churchman but is a corruption of 'fraise', the medieval version of an omelette. It is, in fact, a very early version of apple charlotte.*

**2 large eggs, beaten   1 lb cooking apples, peeled, cored and sliced**
**3 oz butter   3 oz soft brown sugar**
**Rind of half a lemon with 1 teaspoon lemon juice (or ½ teaspoon ground nutmeg)**
**4 oz fresh white breadcrumbs**

Set oven to 375°F or Mark 5. Butter a 1½ to 2 pint pie dish. Cook together the apples, butter, sugar and lemon rind and juice (or the nutmeg), in a saucepan until soft, then beat to make a thick purée. Remove from the heat and stir in the beaten eggs. Spread half the breadcrumbs over the base of the pie dish, spread over the apple mixture and then top with the remaining breadcrumbs. Dot with butter and sprinkle with a little extra sugar and cook for 30 to 40 minutes. Serve hot with custard or cold with whipped cream. Serves 4.

# Breton Eggs

*This is a rather more substantial supper dish, combining sausages,
peas and eggs all cooked together.*

| | |
|---|---|
| **8 eggs** | **1 oz butter** |
| **2½ fl.oz cream** | **3 pork sausages, skinned** |
| **½ teaspoon salt** | **2 thick slices white bread** |
| **½ teaspoon white pepper** | **2 tablespoons cooked peas** |

Put the eggs, cream, salt and pepper in a bowl and beat well together. Parboil the sausages and cut into ½ inch slices. Heat the butter in a pan and fry the sausage slices for about 2 minutes. Cut the bread into ¼ inch squares and add to the pan with the well-drained peas. Cook gently for about 5 minutes, stirring occasionally. Pour in the egg mixture and stir all together until set. Serve on a hot dish garnished with croûtons. Serves 8.

'Feeding the Rabbits' *by C. van Leemputten*

# Egg and Creamed Peas

*An individual serving of a soft boiled egg on a bed of puréed peas and cream, sprinkled with grilled bacon chips. A light, tasty snack.*

| | |
|---|---|
| **6 soft boiled eggs** | **Sprig of mint** |
| **6 rashers streaky bacon** | **¼ pint cream** |
| **1 lb shelled peas** | **Salt and pepper** |

Remove the rind from the bacon and cook under a moderate grill until crisp and crumbly. Set aside and keep warm. Meanwhile, boil the eggs for 5 minutes only and put into cold water to cool. Remove the shells. Boil the peas with the mint until tender, then drain well and liquidise to a purée. Return to the pan, stir in the cream and reheat. Spoon the purée into individual serving bowls, lay a boiled egg on each serving and crumble over the crispy bacon pieces. Serves 6.

# Savoury Baked Eggs

*Finely chopped ham with parsley makes a savoury coating to this simple baked egg starter or light snack.*

**4 eggs**
**Butter, as required**
**4 slices well-buttered toast**

**½ teaspoon finely chopped fresh parsley**
**Salt and pepper**
**2 oz cooked ham, finely chopped**

Set oven to 325°F or Mark 3. Well butter 4 ramekin dishes. Grill 4 slices of toast, butter well and keep warm. Put the ham and parsley into a food processor and chop finely. Use the ham mixture to form a lining pressed on to the buttered sides and bottom of the ramekins. Carefully break an egg into each dish and season with salt and pepper. Bake in a *bain marie* of boiling water until the eggs are just set firm. Turn out each ramekin on to a slice of warm toast and serve. Serves 4.

'A Summer Idyll' *by Walter Hunt*

# Egg and Cheese Pie

*A shortcrust pastry flan case filled with grated cheese and whole eggs, with a crispy breadcrumb topping.*

**4 oz shortcrust pastry**
**4 eggs**
**8 oz Cheddar cheese, grated**
**Salt and pepper**
**1 oz fresh brown breadcrumbs**
**Butter for dotting**
**2 tablespoons milk**

Set oven to 400°F or Mark 6. Grease a 7 inch flan dish. Roll out the pastry on a floured surface, line the dish and trim the edge. Prick the bottom with a fork, line with a circle of greaseproof paper, fill with baking beans and bake blind for about 10 to 12 minutes. Remove the beans and paper, return to the oven and cook for about a further 6 to 8 minutes until baked through. Allow to cool. Reduce oven to 350°F or Mark 4. Spread half the cheese over the base of the flan case and in it make 4 hollows. Carefully break an egg into each hollow and season. Cover with the remaining cheese and then with the breadcrumbs. Dot with butter and sprinkle all over with the milk to moisten. Bake for about 30 to 45 minutes until set and browned on top. Serve with sliced tomatoes. Serves 4.

# Crab Soufflé

*A savoury soufflé which combines crab meat with Parmesan cheese and Cayenne pepper.*

**4 egg yolks   6 egg whites**
**4 tablespoons butter   3 tablespoons flour   ½ pint milk**
**8 oz cooked crab meat**
**6 tablespoons grated Parmesan cheese**
**Salt and Cayenne pepper**

Set oven to 400ºF or Mark 6.  First make a white sauce.  Melt the butter in a pan, stir in the flour and cook for 1 minute.  Remove from the heat and gradually stir in the milk, then return to the heat to thicken, stirring continuously.  When thickened, stir in the crab meat and Parmesan cheese and season with salt and a good teaspoon of Cayenne pepper.  Remove from the heat, allow to cool and then beat in the egg yolks, one at a time.  Meanwhile, beat the egg whites in a bowl until stiff and then gradually fold in to the crab mixture. Butter a soufflé dish, spoon in the mixture and bake for about 20 to 30 minutes until set.  Serve with a green salad.  Serves 4.

# Cornflour Meringue Pudding

*A lemon-flavoured custard pudding with a meringue topping.*

**4 eggs, separated**  
**2 pints milk**  
**1 tablespoon cornflour**  
**4 oz caster sugar**  
**6 drops lemon essence**  
**Pinch of salt**  
**Jam to decorate**

Set oven to 350°F or Mark 4. Butter a large pie dish. Mix the cornflour to a smooth paste using a little of the cold milk. Boil the remaining milk, pour it on to the slaked cornflour and mix together. Return to the pan, bring to the boil and simmer until it thickens, stirring continuously. Remove from the heat and cool slightly. Separate the eggs, beat the yolks in a bowl with 2 oz of the sugar and the lemon essence and stir into the cornflour mixture. Pour the custard into the pie dish and bake for 15 minutes. Meanwhile, beat the egg whites in another bowl with a pinch of salt, to hold their peaks. Fold the remaining 2 oz sugar into the whites and, when the pudding is cooked, heap the egg white on top and return to the oven to brown. Decorate the top with a few dabs of jam and serve hot or cold. Serves 4.

# METRIC CONVERSIONS

The weights, measures and oven temperatures used in the preceding recipes can be easily converted to their metric equivalents. The conversions listed below are only approximate, having been rounded up or down as may be appropriate.

## Weights

| Avoirdupois | Metric |
| --- | --- |
| 1 oz. | just under 30 grams |
| 4 oz. (¼ lb.) | app. 115 grams |
| 8 oz. (½ lb.) | app. 230 grams |
| 1 lb. | 454 grams |

## Liquid Measures

| Imperial | Metric |
| --- | --- |
| 1 tablespoon (liquid only) | 20 millilitres |
| 1 fl. oz. | app. 30 millilitres |
| 1 gill (¼ pt.) | app. 145 millilitres |
| ½ pt. | app. 285 millilitres |
| 1 pt. | app. 570 millilitres |
| 1 qt. | app. 1.140 litres |

## Oven Temperatures

| | °Fahrenheit | Gas Mark | °Celsius |
| --- | --- | --- | --- |
| Slow | 300 | 2 | 150 |
| | 325 | 3 | 170 |
| Moderate | 350 | 4 | 180 |
| | 375 | 5 | 190 |
| | 400 | 6 | 200 |
| Hot | 425 | 7 | 220 |
| | 450 | 8 | 230 |
| | 475 | 9 | 240 |

**Flour as specified in these recipes refers to plain flour unless otherwise described.**